THE
DOG OWNER'S
HANDBOOK

BY MARCUS SCHNECK & JILL CARAVAN

CHARTWELL
BOOKS, INC.

A QUINTET BOOK

ISBN: 0-7858-0334-3

This book was designed and produced by
Quintet Publishing Limited
6, Blundell Street
London N7 9BH

Project Editor: Laura Sandleson
Creative Director: Richard Dewing
Designer: Ian Hunt
Editor: Diana Vowles
Jacket Design: Nik Morley

Typeset in Great Britain by
Central Southern Typesetters, Eastbourne
Manufactured in China by
Regent Publishing Services Limited.

This edition produced for sale in the USA,
its territories and dependencies only.

Published by Chartwell Books
A Division of Book Sales, Inc.
P.O. Box 7100
Edison, New Jersey 08818–7100

Contents

Napoleon, a five-year-old canine, has made his family very unhappy. He runs off whenever he can. He pulls on his leash like Superman proving he's more powerful than a steam locomotive. He refuses to come when called. He growls when anyone touches his toys. He takes food from the table. He barks and growls at everyone. And he has taken over one of the children's beds.

His family are frustrated and are considering having him put to sleep. They say he hasn't learned that he's not the boss – but is he?

Four-year-old Red is very nervous. If he approaches, it's with his head down. Sometimes he has to be coaxed to eat. He hides when the doorbell rings. If anyone raises a voice or a hand, he cringes and rolls over with his feet up.

His family think he's a wimp. They wanted a dog that could act as a watchdog, but this dog is so afraid of everything.

What Napoleon's family don't know is that he sees no reason why he shouldn't be the boss. When he came into the family as a young pup, he wasn't. But he gradually did what any pup would

RIGHT *Submissive behaviour, a product of pack life, is displayed here by the dog rolling over and exposing its underside. The degree to which a dog is submissive is determined by its rank in the pack.*

LEFT *A pack is a group of animals that live together, each dependent on the others for survival. Puppies are born with the pack instinct.*

do – tried to take over and become the dominant member of the family. And they let him.

What Red's family don't know is that he is also reacting to the way they treated him. He may have been a little less aggressive than Napoleon as a pup, but even so, his family obviously never let him get away with anything. His response was to be totally submissive.

Dominance and submission are fundamental components of life for pack animals. Wolves are the quintessential pack animals. And dogs – from the minuscule chihuahua, the smallest dog at 6 inches (15 cm) tall, to the great dane, the largest at 32 inches (81 cm) – are descended from wolves.

THE WOLF PACK

A pack is a group of animals that live together, each dependent on the others for survival. In the wild, the pack supplies protection, companionship, mates, babysitters for the young and hunting companions. Members are loyal and very attached to each other.

Each pack has one leader, usually the most dominant male. He calls all the shots, and everybody else ranks beneath him and must submit to him. Below him, each wolf must be either leader or follower within the rest of the pack.

The leader is often the only male to mate, probably with the "leader" of the female subpack. Because the leader and his mate are the strongest, they will produce strong, healthy offspring. And because no one else is breeding, there won't be too many little mouths to feed. This structure keeps the population manageable, ensuring survival of the fittest.

When male and female leaders have pups, the female becomes the leader of the entire pack until her pups are old enough to travel and hunt with the pack. The sire becomes head wolf again.

Hunting is the reason wolves and dogs are pack animals. They are not fast enough to outrun some prey, so they have joined up in order that they can circle the prey and then attack, leaving no open space for the prey to run to.

Early forebears: Darwin's view

Darwin, the founder of modern evolutionary theory, believed the dog was descended from a mixture of several species of wild Canidae. While this theory is now considered unlikely, there is still something of a mystery about the ancestry of the domestic dog.

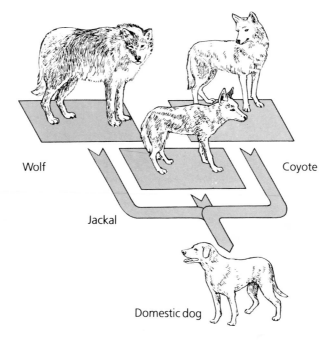

Wolf

Coyote

Jackal

Domestic dog

Once the kill is accomplished, the leader gets to eat first. All the wolves gather around the kill, and if the prey is small, some of the lower-ranking members of the pack may have to wait until higher-ranking members are satisfied and move away from the food.

Because the pack takes care of those who cannot take care of themselves, older wolves are given food if unable to get their own. The lead wolf takes food to his mate while she is raising the pups in the den. Pups are fed by the mother as well as by other adults in the group. They also lick food from the adults' lips, and sometimes the adults regurgitate for the youngsters to eat.

Sometimes the wolves will bury portions of the kill, but usually their stash is found by other animals and the wolves don't reap the benefits.

After the kill and feeding, the pack rests a while, and may spend some time playing. If there is more food in the area, the pack may stay and make the area a home base. The leader will determine when and if the pack moves on. If some members have been separated from the pack during hunting or play, the wolves will howl to gather the pack together.

The leader will retain his position until he is unseated by a stronger, more intelligent wolf or until he dies. There will probably be some fighting among the higher-ranking males to determine who will be the new leader.

A lone wolf cannot survive long without his animal pack. But a dog, even though a pack animal, can survive because he joins a pack of another species – humans.

THE HUMAN PACK

When a dog comes into your family, you take care of all his needs. You provide him with food and shelter, protect him from harm, make sure he is healthy, play with him, and maybe provide him with a mate and help take care of the resulting young.

If he's lucky, you will decide (to a point) what he does and when he does it, and you will be considered top dog. He will receive affection from you, and he will be loving and loyal in return, and it will be a healthy relationship.

When you take a dog into your home, you assume you will be in charge. But if you don't communicate that fact to the dog, in language he understands, he will think he can be leader. You must use consistent discipline to train your dog, but never resort to harsh physical punishment. That would achieve just the opposite, for lead wolves never injure their followers.

If your dog takes over, growls at your every attempt to direct him and even bites you, it

<table>
<tr><td colspan="1">KEEPING A PET</td></tr>
</table>

Do Check that everyone in your home really wants a dog.

Do Be prepared to travel some distance. It is usually only breeders of toy varieties that can be found in big cities.

Do Ask to see the dam of the litter. This will give you an idea of what your pup will look like when full grown.

Do Make sure that the Certificate of Pedigree is in order and that this, and the Form of Transfer, have been signed by the breeder.

Don't Buy a dog if you are out at work all day.

Don't Choose a long-coated breed if you haven't time to groom it.

Don't Buy an Afghan Hound when you really set out to buy a Yorkshire Terrier.

Don't Buy a "pet" quality dog if you plan to exhibit it in pure-bred classes.

ABOVE *Modern dogs expend a lot of energy playing, while their wild ancestors expended their energy hunting down prey for survival.*

won't necessarily be because he's vicious or doesn't love you. It will be because he is a pack animal with pack instincts. But if leadership falls to him instead of you, you've got a dog problem.

If you don't take your place as top dog, he won't necessarily be unhappy, at least directly. But you will be unhappy, which will in turn make life harder for him.

If you take command, his instinct to follow will kick in, and you will have his complete attention while you train him to be a member of your household.

It's not uncomfortable for a dog to be ranked below the leader. Once he realizes he is No. 2 or No. 3 or lower, he will adapt his behaviour accordingly and be happy in that spot.

We misread cues from several family dogs before we actually became comfortable with this fact. Like most animal lovers, we assumed that we were showing our dog love by allowing him to do whatever he wanted (within reason). One look into those puppy-dog eyes, and most humans are pretty much mush when it comes to giving in to a best friend. As individuals with rights and freedoms, we tend to pity any creatures that are in a position to be dominated.

But experience has lived up to research, and we have learned that dogs are happier when they know exactly where they stand. If they have come to accept you as the leader, they will welcome the decisions you make for them and the order you bring to their lives. In fact, most of pack life is devoted to reinforcing each animal's particular position in the pack, even if that turns out to be lowly.

You've had a really hard day. You overslept and got stuck behind a slow wide load on the way to work. Someone was parked in your space, and you had to walk three blocks in the rain without an umbrella.

You lost a filling at lunch, which resulted in an emergency trip to the dentist. You still have a million things to do when you walk in the door. And instead of giving you an understanding hug, your spouse picks a fight with you.

You just can't take any more, so you retreat to your bedroom, feeling as if you don't have a friend in the world, and have a good cry.

That's when Leia appears at your side. She gently reaches out to you with a paw, lays her head on your shoulder, pushes her nose into your face and emits a sympathetic whimper. You're so grateful that you have Leia, who loves you so much that she feels what you feel and wants you to feel better. You have such a wonderful dog.

Well, you probably do have a wonderful dog – but not necessarily because she "loves" you. She may be very attached to you and be very dependent on you. But what she feels for you cannot necessarily be called "love".

But, but . . . what about Lassie? Certainly she loves Timmy. Doesn't Toto love Dorothy? What about Millie and Barbara Bush? Tramp and "My Three Sons"? Astro and George Jetson? Dino and Fred Flintstone? Benji and everybody?

What are all those classic dog stories about if dogs don't love? If Leia doesn't love you, how could she be so adoring, so devoted, so loyal? Unfortunately, she isn't really adoring, devoted or loyal. The love you see in her eyes is all made up in your mind.

BELOW *Because dogs follow the leader of the pack, your dog will want to be where you are, involved in what you are doing, even if he doesn't understand the purpose of your action.*

When Leia exhibits the traits you interpret as love, she is behaving like a pack animal. Dogs do not think or act logically in human terms. It is wrong to expect human actions or reactions from them, and you and the dog will be better off if you learn to treat her as a dog and let her live in harmony with her innate needs.

Because you are the leader, any change in your moods affects your dog. In a wild pack, if the leader snarls and pushes a member of the pack out of the way, the lower-ranking animal will take on a submissive posture and move aside. If the leader cuddles up to another animal and engages in a little relaxed play, there's no reason not to join in and feel that everything's OK.

So if you come home smiling and bubbling, the dog will be elated. If you're miffed at your boss, the dog might be a little more anxious. She would prefer that conditions are always normal. When things aren't, she comes to you in a questioning manner. She wants to be reassured that your out-of-the-ordinary mood is temporary. If you're unhappy, she's unhappy.

This self-concerned behaviour became evident in our house after the first few times we raised our voices to Timber during training. A dog who learns his lessons sometimes too well, he took this one a step further. He knew that a raised voice meant he was in the wrong. But that lesson made him sensitive to any raised voice, even when it isn't directed at him.

We discovered this during a husband-wife argument, when Timber took on a submissive posture and pushed his way on to the wife's lap for reassurance and comfort. (This doesn't mean your dog will always go to the woman in your family for reassurance. The choice of the wife was probably for two reasons. First, in our family, the husband early on took on the role of leader, and the wife filled in as security blanket. Second, the wife's raised voice, although anxiety-producing, is still less threatening than the husband's.)

Loving owners that we are, we stopped arguing and reassured Timber the pack was stable. We have no statistics, but we agree that there have been fewer, or at least shorter, arguments in our family since we discovered Timber's sensitivity.

Just because your dog doesn't exactly love you doesn't mean you can't love her and let her know it. Be sure you don't have any great expectations. Many of us mistakenly treat our pets as children, and because of their dependent nature they end up fulfilling that role. Some people, especially those without children or those who may be recovering from the loss of someone close, have a tendency to use the dog as a substitute child or loved one. You will be sorely disappointed if you expect your dog to give as much as she gets, or if

LEFT *Bonding is a necessary first step in effectively training your dog. When she is secure and confident, she will be happy to approach and learn from you, her leader.*

you subconsciously believe she will always be there, even though you know she probably cannot live more than 10 or 15 years.

Whatever you call it, the two of you can still have a very satisfying relationship. Over time, and with special attempts, you can form a close emotional tie with your dog through bonding.

BONDING

In animal terms, bonding is the pairing of two creatures who develop a long-term connection as the result of shared experiences. It gives animals the desire to stay with each other, to be secure with the other. It is stimulated by face, voice and eye signals, and cooperative behaviour.

Bonding is very pleasant, but it is also a necessary first step in training your dog. When she is secure in the pack, she can be confident in your dealings with her. When she is aware of her place in your life, she feels happy. That can make you happy. And it is much easier for a happy owner to train a happy dog than an unhappy owner to train a dog who is unhappy, fearful and doubtful

MOOD MONITORS

☐ When you bring the dog into your your house, do not crowd or scare her. Gently allow her to look around, and when she seems somewhat at home, bring in members of the family individually and let them handle and talk to the puppy.

☐ Just like a human baby, she won't yet understand what you are saying. But she will be comforted by the tone of your voice. You can change her mood as quickly as you can change your tone. A harsh utterance can snap her out of a playful jaunt, a friendly command can assure that she comes, and some baby talk can elate her.

☐ A lot of bonding involves touch. Your dog will eventually look forward to the way you stroke her fur, pat her head and allow her to fall asleep in your armpit as you stretch out on the couch. Whatever you do as long as it does not hurt the dog, will help you become intimate.

LEFT *Many dogs act jealous by trying to push their way into the family circle when hugs or kisses are exchanged. This is because of their natural desire to maintain their rank in the pack.*

ABOVE *Getting down on a dog's level is a way of making the dog comfortable because he doesn't automatically feel submission due to your largesse. Children have an advantage in this area because their faces are already less threatening.*

she'll squirm away if there's any energy circulating in her frisky body. Then one day, you'll find a lump forming in your throat when your pup actually approaches you for physical contact. A head on your lap, a chin on your ankle, an expectant look into your eyes, a paw on your chest – these are all signs of successful bonding.

If these bonding sessions are welcome, your dog could come to expect them as part of his routine. Our dog Timber, for example, delights in snuggling and then playing with his ball as an after-work bonding ritual.

Bonding also involves introducing the dog to the family's routines. Show her there is a time to play, exercise, eat and sleep. Allow her to keep

of her status. If she bonds with you, she will be very eager to please you.

For a while, you won't get much tenderness in return. Like a toddler who doesn't want to be held – there are just too many toys to play with –

you company as you perform your chores, and take her with you on errands or outings in the motor car if you can.

Playing is especially important for bonding. Get down to her level on the floor. Allow her to "attack" you, roll around, cuddle, run away and make a noise if she wants. Allow her to misbehave during play so she can gain some confidence.

In the animal world, bonding can occur between mates, parent and offspring, or just two middle dogs in the pack. It's best if every member of the family bonds with the dog, and it's OK if everyone's bond is different. The dog will accept whatever relationship arises as long as she knows what to expect. The person who takes the dog for walks, feeds her and accompanies her to the veterinarian may have a different relationship with her than one who merely plays with the dog on occasion, but nevertheless satisfying for both.

At our house, the dog is bonded well enough with the wife that he "pouts" when he sees her getting ready for work. However, since she's

RIGHT *Because your dog is attached to a member of his pack (your family), he may also become attached to things that remind him of the pack through smell or shared experience.*

gone every day, he's over it soon after she leaves. The husband, however, works at home, so the dog depends on his being there most of the time. When he packs a suitcase and leaves the house overnight, the dog spends the evening lying at the front door.

DOGS AND CHILDREN

Most dogs are naturally well disposed toward children and will form a special bond with them. They smell great (to a dog), drop food (eliminates the begging step), have lots of toys (and sometimes they take the dog's), are always active (watch for quick turns) and are short enough to be easy

marks for licking. They also bring out a dog's natural instincts to protect the younger members of the pack.

Of course, not all dogs love all that acitivity. Some breeds are especially good with kids, and others are unenthusiastic or even antagonistic toward them. Dogs who may not have been socialized well can be unpredictable around children. Even a normal dog who has had a bad experience will learn to distrust them. That's why it's important to teach children how to handle a dog.

It's best if the child waits for the dog to come to him or her. Do not make any abrupt move-

LEFT *Dogs are especially attracted to children because they smell great, drop food often, are very active, are easily kissed and have toys to play with.*

ABOVE *Children should never pull a dog's ears, tail, fur or anything else on the dog. Instead, because a dog may react with a display of dominance, they should be taught to wait for the dog to approach them and then touch it gently.*

Even a good-natured dog can react to pain. Give the dog plenty of time for sleep and quiet time. Children can also assist with caring for the dog as a way of bonding.

DOGS AND BABIES

Dogs are especially attracted to babies because they are even more interesting, better smelling and need more protection than older children. The dog's first reaction will be to sniff the baby, which will be OK for both, but be careful about letting her lick because it might scare the baby. Some people also worry about transmission of

ments. Let the dog sniff the back of the child's hand, and if she seems to be friendly, pet her gently.

Never allow a child to pull the dog's ears, tail, fur or anything else that might seem pullable.

germs through a dog's mouth, but this isn't a concern if the dog is clean, vaccinated against germs and free of parasites.

Dogs can become jealous of just about any member of the family, but there is more chance of this in relation to a baby because usually family members are overly concerned about the baby's welfare and tend to notice the dog less.

All dogs will play what are called jealousy games because they react in accordance to pack social rules of dominance and submission behaviour. Dogs that butt in on displays of affection simply feel threatened. They see others getting attention and recognition and join in for fear of being left out. Their natural desire to maintain their rank is what makes them seem so jealous.

RIGHT *The person who takes care of the dog in your house might have a much closer relationship with the dog than someone who just plays with her once in a while.*

LEFT *Fighting between pet dogs may occur when the established dominance relationship changes through illness, or the younger dog grows assertive. There may be a power struggle with fighting over food. The owner must handle the situation carefully.*

DOGS AND OTHER PETS

Another thing that might bring out jealousy in your dog is the way you treat her in relation to other dogs or pets in the household. Your dog will probably assume that she is No. 1 under all the humans in the family, so any other pets should rank below her. Although you probably want to treat all your dogs alike, the dogs need you to choose one to be higher in rank. Always greet, feed and care for that dog first. That reinforces her dominance and lets all the dogs know where they stand. It sounds like the kind of favouritism that humans are always complaining about, but it's what the dogs need.

The owner may be unaware of the established pack order between pet dogs, favouring the underdog – the smaller, older or weaker.

Dog in a Manger

This will upset the natural order, causing the dominant dog to defend its position by attacking the favourite.

The owner should show affection to the dominant dog. The position of both dogs will be defined, the hierarchy accepted.

Our cocker spaniel, Timber, was four months old when we decorated the house for Christmas that year. The Christmas tree went up on a platform next to the window, stockings were hung from the doorway, lights adorned the windows and a strip of silver sleigh bells was hung from the doorknob.

Timber was just about housetrained. He was taken out at regular intervals and seemed to understand the concept. But sometimes he needed to go out between the scheduled outings, and he had not yet figured out how to let us know when.

Some dogs bark or whine, but those things never occurred to him. He knew what to do when we told him to "speak" (especially for food), but he was either too timid or too polite (or too stupid, we sometimes thought) to relate it to asking to go out, even when we suggested it.

Instead, he handled it by getting as close as possible to the port of exit and looking around for someone to lead him outside. Sometimes we'd have that eerie feeling you get when someone's staring at you and we'd look up to see him sitting by the door fixated on one or both of us.

Then one evening we were startled to hear the sleigh bells ring and both ran to see who had dared to open our door without knocking. But the culprit was only Timber, sitting by the door, after having given the sleigh bells a poke. And just for good measure, with his full audience now present, he poked them with his nose again.

BELOW *This dog is telling you that while she is perfectly happy to lie here on the bed with this very comfortable stuffed dog, she is also interested in what the other members of the pack are doing and will change plans if you want.*

Whether he really meant the ring as a signal to go out is still in question, so we're not really bragging about our dog. The point is that we "rewarded" him for the deed by taking him out. So the next time he needed to go out, he rang the bells as a signal to go out.

Ever since then, not just at Christmas, those bells have hung from our front door for Timber to ring when he needs to go out. (In fact, he has a second set on the door at the house of a relative we visit frequently.)

He's four years old now, so he doesn't need as many unscheduled outings as he used to. Three or four times a day is fine for a grown dog. But once in a while, when we've forgotten or lost track of time, we hear the bell ringing.

Not every dog is lucky enough to have bells. All most dogs have is a lot of moving body parts and a few vocalizations, ranging from whimpers to growls to barks and howling. If you listen to your dog, you will gradually learn what each sound and motion means.

VOCALIZATION

Arf, ruff, woof, yip – no matter how you spell it, a bark generally means the dog doesn't know what's going on and is stalling until he can decide (or have a decision made for him) what to do.

If the dog is submissive, a continuous bark when someone approaches the house is directed to the owners. His job, as a lower-ranking member, is to alert you. Reassuring him that you are

LEFT *Barking in this case means "I'm stuck in this fence and I'd really like some help getting out" and should be taken very seriously. While many dog owners hear just one or two types of barking, dogs have a wide variety of barks for different communications.*

21

handling the situation is more effective than anything else to quiet him. A dog who considers himself leader will be more apt to continue barking since it's his territory he's guarding, not yours.

It's usually necessary to note the context of the bark. If the dog barks during a "wrestling" session on the floor, he's probably just excited. If he barks in the car when a vehicle pulls up alongside, he's probably feeling that his personal territory is being invaded. If he barks at birds and other dogs on TV, he's probably somewhere in between those two situations.

Some breeds bark more than others, and some individual dogs bark more than others. Sometimes it depends on the environment in which the dog is raised. A dog living with a retired person might be less prone to noise than one in a family with kids who rough-house a lot. A dog who is teased might bark more than one who is treated with respect and love.

If your dog barks after you give him a command, he is defying you. It may seem cute,

but if you let it go uncorrected, it could be just one step toward his self-election as leader.

No matter how dangerous a barking dog sounds, the adage usually applies that you don't have to worry so much when dogs are barking loudly; they are more threatening when they are quiet or growling.

Growling is more aggressive than barking and should be taken as a warning to stop what you are doing or to keep your present distance. It may be accompanied by a raised upper lip, a crinkled snout and bared teeth, which is prime posture for biting. A lot of growling could be a sign your dog considers himself top dog and feels the need to protect what he thinks he has. Sometimes this happens when the dog has not received constant training and is then suddenly corrected. Alternatively, he may be responding to constant abuse.

Dogs learn that whimpering or whining can get them what they want. The first time we noticed Timber using this tactic, he was sitting

outside the bathroom door looking desperate and whimpering slightly.

Assuming he wanted to get into the bathroom, we opened the door for him. But he only went in and stood by the toilet, whining even louder. When asked what he wanted, he poked his nose at the toilet set and whimpered again. On a hunch, we checked his water bowl; and sure enough, it was empty. When we filled it he took a long drink and went on with his life.

We can't prove that's what he intended, but we now take whimpering seriously at our house. Any time one of his toys gets thrown under furniture or carried into an inaccessible corner by one of our ferrets, Timber whines and points his nose toward it.

Howling is something we usually associate with wolves, but dogs howl, too. In wolf packs the

LEFT Tundra obviously has something to say about the pattern of this quilt her owner is making, in the form of a howl. She probably receives positive feedback for this howling and continues to do it because it seems to please the leader of her pack.

ABOVE Poking his nose into a water source may indicate the dog needs a drink and his water bowl is empty or inaccessible.

howl is an expression of unity – a way of communicating over long distances, to gather the pack, maintain territory or get in the mood for hunting. Your dog may not have the full moon or a ridge in the wilderness to make his howl as eerily romantic as those in literature or films, but if he feels separated from the family, he may embark on a howling session. This separation feeling could come from being left alone in the house too often or simply being locked in another room.

Facial Expressions

Menacing facial expression of the dominant dog.

Submissive pose of a dog which accepts its owner as pack leader.

Howling is so instinctive that dogs tend to join in whenever they hear another dog howling. All the dogs in a former neighbourhood of ours used to get involved in a howling session whenever any of the dogs felt the need. And many house dogs can't resist when they hear a howler on TV.

BODY LANGUAGE

Dogs' next best thing to vocal communication is what they can do with their tails. Sometimes there's so much emotion in the tail that it seems as if it starts at the waist. A wagging tail is said to mean indecision, but if accompanied by a happy face, it probably means the dog is full of joy.

Allowing for differences in conformation according to breed, if the tail is extended horizontally, it indicates contentment; if sticking up, excitement or alertness; if lower between the legs, fear or tension.

Facial expressions are not as easy to interpret. Some owners say they can see when their dogs are "smiling", but people who are not around the dog as much usually think those owners are just one step away from "seeing" UFOs and little green aliens in their back yards. But from two dog owners to others: if you think your dog is smiling, he probably is.

"Smiling", however, has to be taken in context. Your dog probably won't be smiling when being corrected or just after arising. But he might be after chasing a rabbit, in the midst of play or when you get visitors.

Even if he's not smiling, if his ears are poised, his eyebrows raised, his eyes glistening and his movements bouncy, he's probably a pretty pleased pup. If he's just caught his ball from across the room or been praised for obeying a command, he's probably overjoyed.

If his ears are flat and his lip is raised, he may be fearful or uncertain. If his ears are flat and the lips show lots of teeth, he's preparing to attack. If his ears point forward and his muzzle is open, he's ready to attack.

As you can see, ears are crucial to determining expressions. But don't forget to take into account what type of ears your dog has. Ears can range from the pointed ears of the German shepherd to the lop ears of the dachshund. Words such as "raised" or "flat" can mean very different things among breeds.

Unfortunately, some breeds are at a disadvantage because their ears and/or tails are docked. This practice was developed so the ears and tails of hunting dogs could not be easy targets

RIGHT *Dogs' next best thing to vocal communications is what they can do with their tails. This one is sticking up to indicate excitement or alertness, which makes sense since the dog is involved in play.*

for wild animals. Tails were also docked to prevent injuries while the dog was tracking.

Since most cropping is now done because the cropped look has become the breed standard, it might be time to stop. Most dogs are now pets, not trackers and hunters, and docked dogs are hindered in the way they can communicate. If you are waiting for a puppy from a breeder, request that it be totally intact when you pick it up. Otherwise, you may find that cropping has automatically been done.

Another thing dogs have to communicate with is the tongue. Used for lapping up water and food, cleaning and maintaining body temperature,

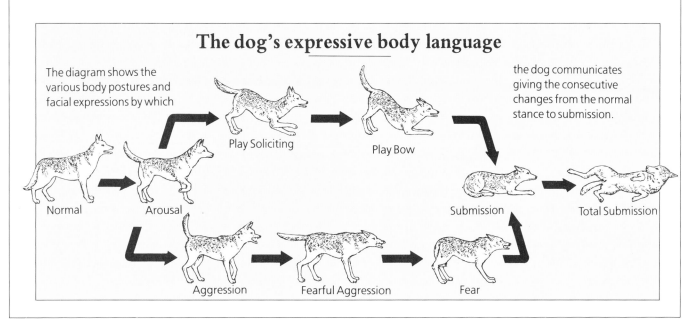

The dog's expressive body language

The diagram shows the various body postures and facial expressions by which

the dog communicates giving the consecutive changes from the normal stance to submission.

Normal

Arousal

Play Soliciting

Play Bow

Submission

Total Submission

Aggression

Fearful Aggression

Fear

it also plays an important role in expressing affection and gratitude.

You may even have been subjected to a "wolf greeting", when the more submissive member of the group greets a more dominant member by nipping, licking and smelling the latter's mouth. In most dogs, this usually ends up just licking because humans tend to discourage the nipping and don't understand the smelling.

Although some people worry about the germs that can be conveyed through this greeting, it has never been proved that diseases are actually transmitted this way. Probably more harm is done to dogs when they are told they cannot greet in this manner; they react by feeling separation from, and insecurity within, the pack.

We are among the dog owners who have been criticized for "spoiling" our dog and "treating him like a child" by letting him do this and other instinctive actions that meet with disapproval. But we are treating him more like the pack animal he is than do those who deny his true needs.

DOG LANGUAGE

Here are a few other things you might need to know about what your dog is telling you, directly or indirectly:

☐ When your dog lies on his back, his underside totally exposed, he is proving his submission to you.

☐ Dogs have sweat glands all over their bodies, but full cooling occurs only by the movement of air over the dog's wet tongue. That's why water is so important for your dog. If he refuses to answer a command and is panting, he may be telling you he needs a little time off.

☐ A dog sprawled flat on the floor is not necessarily suffering from heat or exhaustion. He may also be showing you he is relaxed and content.

☐ When a dog gives you his paw without prompting, he may be asking for something. This action is instinctive in dogs, as they learned early on that kneading their mother's teats stimulated the flow of milk. As adults, this becomes a begging gesture. This explains why it's so easy for most dogs to learn to "shake".

☐ Jumping on a wolf who comes home with a kill is normal behaviour for pack animals. That's why a dog might jump on you as you enter, especially if he smells groceries or a new toy.

☐ In the wild, only the lead dog makes direct eye contact. Dogs have learned they can make eye contact with humans even if they are submissive. But if yours combines eye contact with growling or some other aggressive behaviour, he may be telling you he's feeling a little dominant.

There is a gag in use among many cartoonists – we believe we first saw it in a "Far Side" cartoon by Gary Larson – that depicts a man and his dog, Ginger, in conversation.

The man, very agitated, is saying something like "Ginger, I'm really upset with you. That was a perfectly good shoe. But look at what you did to it. It looks like some of your leftover food that's been sitting around for days."

The dog, smiling and content, is actually hearing "GINGER, blah, blah blah-blah blah blah. Blah blah blah blah-blah-blah GOOD blah. Blah blah blah blah blah blah blah-blah blah FOOD."

In other words, Ginger is understanding only three words: "Ginger", her name; "good", which the man usually uses to mean he is pleased with something that Ginger has done; and "food", which Ginger has learned to mean something good to eat. So the message the dog is actually putting together from all this is, "Ginger, good, food" – a message quite different from what the man intended.

RIGHT *Dogs learn to recognize their name and other important words through repitition, and will comprehend their words even in other contexts.*

LEFT *Regular exercise off the leash will help to prevent a young dog from becoming destructive around the home. Here a young labrador is retrieving an object for its owner.*

RIGHT *Be careful of what signals you are giving your dog while training. He understands commands literally and because he looks for cues he may pick up nuances you never intended for him to obey.*

As exaggerated as this cartoon example may be, none of us who has lived with a dog can deny the reality of it. Dogs may not understand English as a language, but they can learn to understand some words in whatever language their owners speak, and all the junk we put around the key words falls on deaf ears.

We have joked about how much fun it would be to teach dogs the wrong meaning of words – "go", for example, when we mean come, "come" when we mean "sit" or "run" when we mean him to speak – or even nonsense words for all his commands – "plant" for sit, "pudding" for come or "supercalafragilistic" or some such word for roll over.

We didn't actually do that, for the same reason you don't name your dog something like "Edward" – it's not the kind of word you want to be yelling from the back door when you call the dog. Nor do you want your dog to look stupid when you tell it to "fetch" and it rolls over. But the concept does show that dogs learn the meanings you teach them.

We tried just about everything to make our puppy grasp the concept of "Come!" – praise . . . pushing him across the room . . . pulling his leash . . . treats . . . and finally enticing him with Oogie, his favourite tug toy.

Oogie did the trick. He simply couldn't resist "coming" when he saw the latex dog face that he had had the pleasure of sniffing out and un-wrapping for Christmas. We used it to reel him in to the "come" command, and rewarded him with a tug session at Oogie's expense.

Sometimes we tried it without Oogie, and he was reluctant, but always agreeable in the end. We had finally trained him to come. Our complacency lasted only a few weeks. One day when asked to come, he took a little side trip to pick up Oogie along the way. Apparently, the dog perceived our reward as our intent, and so when we stopped using Oogie, he felt something was missing and tried to recapture that pleasure.

For months, no matter where the object was, the dog would run to fetch a toy on his way – even after he traded in Oogie for a rubber ball as the toy of choice.

Only after months of training with commands like "no", "now" and "just you" did he learn that "come" doesn't always mean "bring your ball here". Even today, he still slips up and grabs the ball if it's at his feet as we say "Come!"

The moral of the story is be careful what signals you give while training. Your dog does "understand" commands, but not according to the dictionary definition.

Through repetition, your dog will come to associate events, actions or objects with specific sounds and words. This is how a dog learns to recognize his own name and words that mean important things.

If you say "walk" enough times as you take the dog out for one or pick up her leash, she will get to know what it means. Even if you say it in some other context, the dog will think you mean her and whip her head around to show interest.

Your dog loves to hear you talk even when not giving commands, especially if you say nice things in a nice tone of voice. She will especially go for that high-pitched baby talk that many people use with dogs because animals in the wild communicate in a high-pitched tone if they are friendly. She will not like your deeper tone because animals in the wild communicate in lower tones if they are aggressive.

Your tone can say a lot even if she doesn't get a clue about the context. Some dogs react to any raised voice, even one not directed at them, by cowering or seeking comfort. Dogs who hear pleasant conversation will be relaxed.

You will need three voices to communicate with your dog: a firm, gentle voice for commands, a yelling voice for correcting and a baby-talk voice for praise and bonding. Use the correct voice in context since dogs will read these signals as they are given.

SIGNALS AND BODY LANGUAGE

The art of detecting signals from humans is born from the way members of a pack interact, using sounds and body language to express emotions and wishes. Because of this previous "experience", your dog also picks up body language from you, opening the way for training, either intentionally or unintentionally, with hand signals and other cues you might display.

These non-verbal leads are almost a necessity for dogs learning to work in films, on television or in other areas of the entertainment field. Sometimes they have to work at a distance from the trainers, or the trainers have to be "quiet on the set" during filming but still get the dog to do what her part requires.

The dog may also learn to pick up non-verbal cues that we never intended. When we carry ourselves too casually, loosely gripping the leash, a dog with a tendency toward aggressiveness may try to take control. When you hold the leash securely and walk confidently, the dog gets a more positive message.

Some dogs, however, are intimidated by too much authority in posture and will react by being overly submissive. The average person already towers above a small dog, preventing her from making facial contact, so it's best to stand a foot or so away and get down to her level sometimes.

Your hands should be used only for actions that your dog will associate with positive bonding: petting, scratching, hugging, feeding, playing and training. Never use your hands to hit the dog or hold its muzzle shut or anything else the dog might interpret as aggressive.

If a dog backs off when hands reach out to her, she has probably been abused. Assure her she is in no danger in your household. You want the dog to trust you, but don't expect miracles overnight. It is a long process.

When touching this type of dog, bring your hand up from the ground, palm up, starting with the underside of her chin, or offer your knuckles to her nose for sniffing. Never reach out to her in a manner that makes her think your hand is coming toward her (especially from above) to hit her as it will only frighten her.

Only the lead dog makes direct eye contact in the wild, but dogs have learned they can make eye contact with humans even if they are submissive. Be sure you are not accompanying your glare with unfriendly postures. Most dogs can handle the posture or the eye contact, but put one with the other and add a human growl, and some dogs will be truly frightened. This might sound like fun, but if you do it too often, you could erode the bond you have made with your friend. Some dogs react by being totally submissive and urinating uncontrollably.

On the other hand, if you need to quiet a dog, this might work. But beware that an aggressive dog may be provoked to attack.

We also tell our dogs a lot of things we never mean to by our actions. Throwing off a blanket in the morning can mean getting out of bed. Putting on a coat means someone's going outside. A suitcase by the door means someone's going away overnight.

BELOW *You will need three voices that replicate tones that dogs use among themselves to communicate with your dog: firm for commands, loud for corrections and "baby talk" for praise and bonding.*

One summer a relative was planning to look after Timber while we went on vacation. "Will he listen to me?" she asked. "What do I say to him to make him behave?"

To assure that she would be in control (which we knew would also be better for the dog in the long run) and that our best friend would feel secure in his temporary environment, we wrote down a few commands

The list is not to show you what a wonderful dog we have. It's to show the potential for dogs to learn commands. In all honesty, we planned to stop after the usual few, but after we learned how quickly he picked up words on his own it became fun to see what he was capable of.

Since we raised him like a submissive pack animal, he spends most of his time looking to us for cues and commands. It may seem like a

LEFT *"Release" is the command this hunter uses to ask this German shorthaired pointer to give up the quail it has just delivered. It's also a good command for the surrender of toys and other objects.*

shallow existence to humans, who have hopes and dreams and egos, but nothing makes the dog happier than pleasing you. If you let him, he will spend his entire life (except when he's exhausted) making sure he is doing what you want.

He's comfortable in this position because of his heritage as a pack animal. In the wild, wolves cater to the wishes of the leader: they eat when he eats, hunt when he hunts, sleep when he sleeps, get out of his way when he wants them to and play when he initiates it.

Dog owners are sometimes criticized for this type of behaviour in their dogs. "You might as well be confining him in a cage for his whole life", the critics say. But if they really knew dogs, they'd know they're arguing for their own needs, not the dog's. Of course, you have to know how to train your dog to attain this kind of relationship. It doesn't just happen.

TRAINING

Training can begin at approximately seven weeks. First the dog has to get used to his collar and leash. Try the collar first without the leash, and then a few days later attach the leash and let him drag it around for a period each day.

Only one family member, preferably the dog's leader, should train the dog at first. Be aware of your tone of voice, your hand signals and posture, your dog's personality and your dog's mood.

Experts recommend three tones of voice for dealing with a dog: a firm voice, used normally and for commands; a yelling voice, for correcting, and a baby-talk voice, for praise and bonding. Most dogs respond attentively to the normal voice, with submission to the yelling voice and elation to the baby-talk voice.

Training denies your dog every impulse that is natural for him, so it may take him a while to

RIGHT *You can teach your dog to ask for whatever he wants by using commands like "sit", "up", "speak", and "shake".*

LEFT *This tiny poodle cross puppy is just beginning to understand the meaning of "come" and will gladly do so if he remains submissive.*

hear your commands and understand your goal. It can take up to three sessions for a dog to respond to a new command.

If you use hand signals correctly, your dog will learn a separate hand signal for every command. Eventually the hand signals can be used alone, so choose hand signals you can live with.

If the dog is affectionate, you'll be able to use affection as a reward. If he is more aggressive, be firmer. However, no matter what his temperament, the time to train him is not when he is tired. You can tell by noticing what else is hap-

pening in the room, too. If there are children or other pets, or someone is putting on a coat to go out, your dog will be distracted.

Unless your dog is in advanced training for obedience trials or showing, sessions should be limited to 15 minutes. He will enjoy learning new commands and tricks, but because repetition over a period is the key, there's only so much he can learn in one day, anyway. His attention span is such that he bores easily unless he gets a break. Because training tends to tax a dog so much, he will probably want to nap soon after each session.

THE COMMANDS

Name The first thing you should teach your dog is his name. He won't ever really understand the concept of a name as such, but he will know that when you say that word you want his attention. If you use his name when you talk to him, he will learn it. When he responds, praise him.

Sit To teach "sit", hold the dog on his leash so he must hold his head up. Then, as you say the word, push his rump down. After a time, just moving your hand over his head and saying the word should do it. If your dog needs more incentive, hold a treat instead of the leash over his head.

BELOW *At the end of a training session, always remember to pat the dog and give words of praise.*

The Command "Sit"

With the dog standing still, give the command "sit". Gentle pressure over the hindquarters as shown may first be necessary to evoke the required response.

Sitting is a natural posture for dogs and they should feel quite happy in this position.

You should be able to kneel down, keeping the leash held high, without upsetting your dog.

Lie down We have found that dogs have a really tough time understanding the concept of "lie down" from a standing start. You'll find it easier if he is seated. Then push down on his neck until he lies down. If you have to, pull his front legs forward. If he tries to get up, repeat the command and push down on his back.

Stay "Stay" is a command that can save the dog's life, above and beyond being obedient. It can assure that he sits at the kerb as traffic goes by, for example.

Once the dog has learned "lie down" or "sit", "stay" is the next step. Tell the sitting or lying dog to "stay" and then move away a little. If he gets up, push him down and repeat "stay". Increase the distance each day. When he stays even when you are out of sight, he deserves more reward. If he has a tough time with this one, use his leash, and as the person in front moves away, the person behind him holds him back.

Come If your dog is going to be outside without a leash, "come" is crucial. Teach it inside and

ABOVE *Training is a sequence of lessons, and at this stage you can move back towards the dog and slip off its leash. Always leave the collar on under these circumstances so that you can restrain the dog more easily, if it attempts to run off.*

LEFT *Once the dog is sitting, you can then extend the leash on the ground. Hand signals are an important part of the trainer's repertoire, the raised hand here indicating "stay."*

The Command "Lie down"

The dog should then be reasonably comfortable. It is best to carry out this exercise in the home, or on a dry patch of grass so that the dog can rest happily.

The command "down" is especially important for large dogs, so that they do not cause problems in the home. From the sitting position the dog's front legs will need to be lowered, as shown here.

Using a hand signal to show that you want the dog to stay in position, you can give further encouragement by holding on to the leash in the early stages of reaching this command.

Lhamar, a 12-week-old lhasa apso puppy, is learning to get used to his collar. Once he does, he can move on to command training.

If you use hand signals in conjunction with voice commands, your dog may eventually learn to follow the hand signals without ever hearing the command.

then move outside. This works best with two people. One holds the dog from behind and the other goes across the room and tells the dog to come. The dog will be thrilled if you get down on his level and will be more inclined to come to someone he can actually reach. If bonding has been pleasant, he may come without incentives. If he needs motivation, hold a treat or, using the leash, pull him over when you give the command and praise him when he arrives. Start not more than a few feet from the pup, and gradually increase the distance.

Once he has grasped this concept inside, try it outside, but definitely use the leash out there to ensure he doesn't run off and get into trouble.

Never call your puppy to come when you plan to punish him. He will associate coming to you with being punished and will see this as a reason not to come to you.

No Use "no" whenever you want your dog to stop doing something. Say it at the crucial time. After the dog has jumped off the couch is no time to give him a "no" for being on the furniture. "No" at that point applies to getting off the furniture. If you've said "no" at the right time before, he knows you don't want him *on* the couch; now you tell him you don't want him getting *off* the couch. At this point he's more confused than anything – see why timing is so important?

If you watch your dog carefully when he's close to doing something wrong, you're likely to catch him before he acts, which is the appropriate time for "no". Wait until he has obeyed the command, and then praise him for doing so. His mother did something similar when she showed him what actions she disapproved of by making a noise or a motion to deter him.

When issuing positive commands it helps to use the dog's name followed by the command. However, if you use "no" with the dog's name he may come to associate his name with a negative. So be careful.

Release When you say "release" or "let go" to a puppy, he should let you take away whatever he is playing with. At first he will growl and defend his possession, which is how he behaved with his litter mates when he had to assert himself for whatever he could get. Even though it's a natural reaction he needs to be deterred, or he will refuse to surrender some object that may harm him or some expensive sweater you bought for a special occasion. It's much easier to teach this to a puppy with baby teeth than an adult with larger teeth.

Practise this with his toys and food, so he doesn't have to learn in a state of emergency. Be sure to praise the dog for giving up what he is guarding so closely. After a while he will come to think of it as a natural response because it pleases you, his leader.

LEFT *"Stay" is probably the command these dogs were given to make them wait on the back of this truck until their owner comes out of the store.*

OK Use "OK" when you want him to know he is released from whatever discipline you previously expected of him. When Timber is told to "wait" while we set food down for him, "OK" is what releases him to eat the food. When he has "come", but he gives you that look that says he wants to be somewhere else, "OK" lets him know when he can leave.

"OK" can also be used to show that everything is all right – after he is attacked by another dog, for example, or if he's feeling sensitive to arguing voices. Don't say "OK" though if everything really isn't, or he'll learn not to trust your word.

Heel Even if your dog is always on a leash, heeling is important. If he doesn't heel then, he'll be dragging you along by the leash.

Let the puppy get used to the collar and leash before you ever venture outside. First let him drag the leash around for limited periods for a few days and then start holding it and walking with him. Talk to him when you do this so he will connect the leash with you being pleasant and see it as a point of contact with you.

The next step is to take him outside. Once he is accustomed to this, start teaching him the "heel" command, keeping the leash short so he has to stay by your side and pulling back on him if he tries to get ahead of you.

We use the term "right here" for Timber because it works in the house, too, when we need him at a certain spot. The actual word you use is not as important as letting your dog know what you mean. If possible, give your dog a chance sometimes to run off excess energy without the leash. It will be almost as much fun for you as it is for him as you watch him bouncing around tracking squirrels and rabbits.

TRICKS

"Does he know any tricks?" is a question other people tend to ask about your dog. Tricks are those things your dog does on command that aren't for manners or safety reasons. You probably don't want your dog to know as many tricks as a circus animal or a dog who "acts" in the movies, but it can be fun to learn some things beyond the basics. As long as there is no abuse involved in the tricks you teach your dog, he will enjoy learning at this advanced level because it keeps him occupied, allows him to spend more time with you and pleases you.

The following tricks are not those your dog needs to know for a dog show. Nor are the commands above given according to show standards. If you want to train your dog for showing, check with the appropriate breeding organization for standards. However, if you just want to enjoy your dog, here are a few primary tricks to try.

BELOW *A dog who really enjoys "fetch", as well as swimming, can be trained to combine the two passions.*

Speak First make him sit, then hold up food slightly over his head and tell him to speak. You may need also to use "wait" or "stay" to keep him from jumping up. If he doesn't understand, bark once yourself. After a while he might try to combine sit and speak when he sees the food.

Shake Put your hand out while saying "shake", and if necessary, put his paw on your hand. Food rewards help this one along.

Roll over Not the easiest thing to teach a dog who likes to keep his feet on the ground.

Command him to lie down then, using food, trace a circle in the air to the side you want him to roll to, helping him along with a gentle push, first on to his back, then over on to his other side, and finally into the lying position again.

BELOW *Tricks like "up" are easy to train when the dog is given food as a reward. Dogs see food as a reward because their acceptance in the wild pack means they get to share in the food of the pack.*

PRAISE

While the dog is mastering his commands, you have to master praise. As you show your dog what you want, praise him so he knows what he can expect. The first time he performs correctly, reinforce his behaviour with a special treat (but work out these treat calories in relation to the dog's daily intake). Once the dog has mastered the lessons, the treats can be phased out. Eventually, praise will be enough.

Praise can make some dogs feel that they can return to what they want to be doing, so give just enough to let him know you are pleased with what he has done – don't overdo it.

In the area of feeding, more than in any other area of dog behaviour, the relationship we have established with our dogs is one that makes them remain "puppies". They may look like adult dogs, but like Peter Pan, they never quite take over all the responsibility of being an adult – in this case, finding their own food.

Puppies in the wild are first fed mother's milk and are later fed from the kill by her and the other adult members of the pack. At first the pups cannot chew their own meat, so the adults eat it then regurgitate it, partially digested, for the pups to eat in more liquid form. When the pups are able to chew, they are given pieces by the adults. When they are adults themselves, they will give food to elderly members of the pack as well as the new pack pups.

In our homes, pups are provided for just as they are in the wild. We may not regurgitate, but we teach our pups that all food comes from us and we never allow them to gather their own food. In that sense, they may "feel" like puppies all their lives, which is probably to our advantage because it helps them to see themselves as lower-ranking members of our pack.

Even so, they take an active interest in the provision of that food. Whoever comes in the door with grocery bags is usually greeted in much the same way an adult wolf would be met on coming "home" with a recent kill. While cooking is in progress the dog will take up position in the kitchen just as he would if he were a lower-ranking member of the pack – not allowed to touch the food, but nevertheless waiting for his

LEFT *When your dog exhibits the traits you interpret as love, she is merely behaving like the pack animal she is.*

BELOW *Domestic dogs remain puppies all their lives in the sense that they are always dependent on the human adults in their packs for food. In the wild, they would have a chance to mature in this manner.*

turn. This behaviour carries over to the dinner table, where he needs to be if there is a possibility of his getting access to the food.

BEGGING

Begging is a natural extension of this, as it is customary for wolves to "beg" adults for food. Because they are permitted to lick what's left on the adults' lips, don't be surprised if your pooch tends to notice that you have spaghetti sauce on your shirt or a milk moustache. If you allow your dog to beg, you will want to take great care that his breath is good because the idea of begging in the wild is to make sure the adults see you and pay attention to your needs. Your begging dog will do everything possible to make sure he is in your field of vision, even if it means resting his head on the table, breathing on your food, waving his paws at you and bargaining with (temporary) gifts of his toys. (Wolves give sticks and bones in the wild as a submission ritual.)

If your dog's attentive he'll even learn who is and isn't a soft touch and, of those targets, who has to be begged at first because they eat faster than the others. Some dogs won't even rest after you have finished eating. If they know there is food left out anywhere, they beg until it's all gone.

Most people do not appreciate begging, so you might want to deter your dog from doing it. Feed your dog before sitting down to your own meal. Allow him to eat only from his own bowl. Never give him between-meal treats. If your pup needs more to get the message, say "no" when he comes near you to beg. Use a corrective jerk of his leash if necessary.

DIET

You probably won't go wrong feeding your dog commercially prepared foods. Housetraining is more easily regulated in some dogs if they are on dry food, although to avoid allergies and harmful chemicals a natural food is sometimes best.

MEALTIME TIPS

☐ If you feed a dog late at night you only have yourself to blame if the dish is not clean until morning.

☐ It does not matter whether you feed your adult dog once a day, or twice, dividing the food ration into two portions. However, toy breeds with small stomachs often fare better on two or even three little meals a day.

☐ On average a dog weighing 10 lb (4.5 kg) needs 8 oz (225 g) of food a day. A dog weighing about 25 lb (11 kg) needs 1¼ lb (565 g).

☐ Never ever give your dog poultry bones. They could be swallowed whole and splinter inside its stomach.

Most people assume dogs are solely carnivores (meat-eaters) because their wolf ancestors only eat meat. But wolves also eat the partially digested food in the stomach of their herbivorous (plant-eating) prey, which gives them the remaining nutrients they need. A modern diet for the domestic dog may include cereals, rice, vegetables and fruit. Breeders and veterinarians used to recommend a raw egg for a good coat, but in these days of rampant salmonella, raw eggs are not advised. Depending on how active the dog is, the proportion of fat in the diet should be no more than 20–25 per cent.

It's natural for humans to want to respond to dogs' need for food by feeding them whatever and whenever they want – and they will eat as much as they can if they like the food. A healthy adult wolf can eat 20 lb (9 kg) of meat at one feeding. He will also test his powers of swallowing. Adult wolves have been known to "wolf down" an entire caribou tongue in a gulp. However, you're not showing true love for your pet if you're just making him overweight and suscep-

LEFT *Dogs have been known to eat tissues, pebbles, toys, paper and maybe even, in the case of this dog, something that washed up on the beach. He doesn't understand that he does not live in the natural world and may be endangering himself.*

RIGHT *This photograph seems to illustrate how dogs spend approximately 80 per cent of their waking hours, thinking about food, a throwback to wild instincts that tell the dog to always be on the lookout for food sources.*

Hide and seek

If dogs do not eat all their food at once, they frequently cache what is left over; both wild and domestic dogs do this and the most common example of it is the burying of the bone. Any food which is surplus to immediate requirements is likely to be hidden where the dog can easily find it again. Unlike cats, most dogs seem prepared to eat meat that is high almost to the point of rotting.

Foxes will carry the food to be cached to a selected spot.

The food is held in the mouth while a shallow hole is dug.

Soil is replaced over the cache by long sweeps of the nose.

tible to health problems. If your dog is already obese, he needs to be on a strict schedule for feeding and exercise.

Despite the canine reputation for gorging, some dogs act finicky. In highly strung dogs, this may signal a nervous stomach. In dogs bordering on aggressive, it may be a holdout tactic for food they like better – i.e., what is on their owners' plates. Don't let them convince you that they will starve if they don't eat right away – they are well prepared to live off a recent meal for a few days. Wolves can survive up to two weeks without eating.

Don't get caught up in believing your dog is loyal because you feed him, either. Dogs are loyal because you are the leader and offer them companionship, not because you feed them.

No matter what or when you feed your dog, because of his preoccupation with food he will probably be unable to resist food odours from your rubbish bin unless you have trained him that rooting through the rubbish displeases you.

Another unattractive habit your dog may have is eating faeces or his own vomit. Although it's disgusting to humans, for dogs it's a survival instinct. In the den, the mother licks up her pups' waste, just as she ate the afterbirth when they were born. Removing any traces of them ensures their protection from predators. However, along with being an unacceptable habit in a human household, it also puts the dog in danger of picking up parasites from another animal.

Dogs have also been known to eat tissues, pebbles, toys and paper. If a trend develops, have a veterinarian check your dog out because the need to eat strange objects could be the result of an enzyme deficiency.

Dogs also have a habit of burying bones and leftover food as a carryover from when their species needed to do this to store food for later. Although our domesticated canines are rarely in danger of starvation, they have been unable to shed this instinct and might end up digging in your garden to follow it.